This book belongs to:

_____

Praise for *OCEANS!*

"I love it!!! It's easy to read, rhythmic, colorful, and engaging. As an educator I can say this book is GREAT for word recognition/identification, letter recognition, pattern recognition, attention to detail, and ability to gather information from text or illustrations (investigation, research). This book is also a great tool to prompt and reinforce those skills while engaging the student and teaching content (science). As a parent of a son who had to be bribed to read (elementary years), I can say this book is a game changer. The illustrations are fantastic!"

— Liddy Zarone, M.S., NCC, Professional School Counselor

"I love the artistry and the message the book is sharing with children. The interactive nature of this book is really great for young learners. They receive small amounts of information and then an activity to work on with each page. This gives children time to process the information the book shares, and a reason to keep coming back to the pages, so many awesome details, there is no way to enjoy it all in one sitting. The facts shared about our beautiful oceans are really high interest and add to the story of protecting them. I am lucky to have been able to read this story and can't wait to share it with my own young learners."

— Georgia Kavina, MAT, 7th Grade Life Science Teacher, Science Lead Teacher

"Oceans! is not your ordinary seek and find book. This one is delightful and colorful, but also educates readers of all ages about the mysteries of the ocean. After reading, a secret message is revealed and bonus features are added to continue the seek and find adventure. The author's love of the ocean and zeal for education clearly shine through in this exceptionally entertaining book. It is as fun as it is educational."

— Elaine G. Hudson, Ed.S - Student Placement Coordinator

"Clearly written and illustrated to engage young readers . . . and their elders! Important information is offered in a fun format. Colorful and humorous illustrations entertain and provide more information. The farther you read, the more you learn. A fun read on an important topic."

— Sue Thompson, M.Ed., (ret.) Learning Disabilities Educator

"A completely unique and wonderful book. Perfect in a teacher's classroom, a child's bedroom, or even English as a Second Language (ESL) classes, with the rhyming words and interactive exercises. Delightful illustrations perfectly illuminate the words on each page. In other children's books, words and illustrations aren't integrated; in this book, the author and illustrator worked in concert. You can tell. "Oceans!" is pleasurable to look at, over and over…there is always something new and fun that catches the reader's eye. It's a shrewd combination of artistry, humor, and learning."

— Saralyn Aylor, M.Ed,. Instructional Supervisor, World Language and ESL

"WOW!!!!! It engages readers, both young and old, in the learning and teaching about our precious oceans and the call to our careful stewardship of God's creation. This multi-sensory approach makes way for the variety of learners who will read it. It will be a real asset to the literacy program in which I'm involved through our church's outreach and education program."

— *Pastor M.K. Huntsman, Altavista Outreach and Enrichment Program, Altavista UMC, Altavista, VA*

"I love this book! It is bright, colourful, VERY engaging, and will provide hours of fun reading it, searching for all the wonderful hidden items, AND learning some very interesting facts about our oceans. Sure to entertain, educate, and delight in equal measure - I certainly learned a few things, and I thoroughly enjoyed whiling away the time searching for some particularly well-hidden secret objects!"

— *Keith Blakemore-Noble, UK's #1 Fear Strategist*

"This book is a 'must have' on the shelves in every home. The author has written an interactive book that will be enjoyed by generations now and yet to come. Factual research is clear and concise. The reader's attention is kept on the subject of Oceans, while the 'Seek and Find' format makes each page a thrill. Illustrator Gus Morais has accomplished so much, with fabulous art on each page that brings the words to life. As I read it to my grandchildren and watch them navigate the questions and answers at the end, it will be a joy to watch them learn."

— *Diane McLaughlin, Nonna to Ben, Kate and Mason*

"Kids enjoying this book can stay busy for hours – parents, did you hear that? HOURS. The entertainment doesn't get boring because there are different things to do throughout the book, rather than having 79 search and find puzzles in a row. Also, regular search-and-find books don't teach. This one does."

— *James Detrick, Grandpa to RosieMae and Joshua*

"A fun and whimsical look at the oceans - a book that will surely inspire future marine biologists!"

—*Tim Schul, Dad to Hannah, David and Sarah*

"An environmentally-aware search-and-find treasure, this delightful book offers hours of educational fun to young readers. Its gloriously detailed and playful illustrations are humorously captivating: every time your child picks it up, they will find something new. From spotting and learning the names of common and rare sea creatures, to a Bonus Features section including 'Facts about the Oceans', this book educates while promoting environmental awareness and personal responsibility - so your child will be learning and gaining a sense of global citizenship, all while having fun."

— *Stephanie Katavolos, Mom to Leo and Tabitha*

"I wish I'd had books like this when I was growing up."

-- *Jake Fulkerson, the author's son and original inspiration behind the Kayful Books concept*

OCEANS!

A KAYFUL BOOKS SEEK - AND - FIND ADVENTURE

Written by Karen Fulkerson
Illustrated by Gus Morais

Story copyright © 2019 Karen Fulkerson
Illustrations copyright © 2019 Gus Morais

ISBN: 978-1-947486-12-6

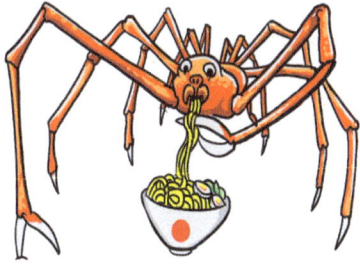

For Bruce, Jake, Meredith, Gus, my family, friends and IG/FB followers: thank you.

Also, for teachers everywhere: You are wonderful! Let's Go!

Oceans are full of animals and plants; the waters are salty and deep.
They cover a lot of our planet, and millions of secrets they keep.

SHARKS ARE FRIENDS

OCEANS

STOP!

Some oceans are warm and some are cold. They're found all over the earth.
There isn't a way for us to measure their beauty and their worth.

*On these pages, find the Magic Word "OCEANS", a jellyfish, a rainbow parrotfish,
a banana boat, and a fish in a hammock!*

Oceans are habitats with big and small creatures! That blue whale must eat like a pig!
He's the largest animal found on the earth! How does he get so big?

The blue whale eats tiny shrimp called krill. He can eat four tons each day. This big blue giant eats itty bitty shrimp, and hundreds of tons he can weigh.

On these pages, find the Magic Word "WE", a fangtooth fish, a spotted eagle ray, a Picasso triggerfish, and a diver offering a shark a huge drumstick!

SOS

Ocean waters dance; they never stay still. The waters move and they churn.
Sit near the ocean, but protect your skin, or you could get a painful sunburn.

The ocean has tides, both low and high, that happen because of the moon.
The tide is "low" when the sea is "out"; don't fret, it'll come back in soon!

*On these pages, find the Magic Word "PROTECT", a fish-shaped pond, a crabby
constellation of stars, a pelican, and a fish who loves to surf!*

PROTECT

More animals in the ocean? Yes! Mammals and fish. Reptiles and mollusks, too.
Seals, otters, dolphins and whales are mammals; they're all in the ocean, so blue.

Fish include sharks, eels, swordfish and rays…tuna, grouper and flounder, as well. Squid, octopuses, and snails are mollusks, of course; some don't, but some do, have a shell.

*On these pages, find the Magic Word "TO", a seahorse, a swordfish,
a golden treasure chest, and a fish using some binoculars!*

In the ocean you might find some jellyfish, or maybe anemones!
Both look so amazing, but do not touch; their stingers cause injuries.

Sea turtles are reptiles that swim in saltwater. Sea snakes are reptiles, too.
Saltwater crocodiles live near the beach, very close to the ocean, it's true!

*On these pages, find the Magic Word "OUR", a sea snail, a sea turtle,
a saltwater crocodile, and a crab holding onto a girl's hair!*

FISH RACE

Plants in the ocean make air that we breathe; to damage them would be unjust.
Seaweed and mangroves, kelp and seagrasses; it's our job to protect them. We must!

Ocean plants protect baby creatures, which bigger fish want to be catching.
As long as these plants are healthy and growing, sea critters will keep on hatching.

*On these pages, find the Magic Word "NEED", a sea otter, a boy in a skeleton costume,
some fish hiding among seagrasses, and a puppy driving a submarine!*

THE GREAT UNDERWATER AQUARIUM

RENT A SUB

DO YOU NEED A SUBMARINE?

Oceans are full of animals and plants; the waters are salty and deep.
They cover a lot of our planet, and millions of secrets they keep.

Some oceans are warm and some are cold. They're found all over the earth.
There isn't a way for us to measure their beauty and their worth.

*On these pages, find a sea lion, a baby snow seal, an igloo,
a person wearing skis, and a fish ice-skating!*

TITANIC

Below, write the six magic words from each of the pages...

_____

_____

_____

_____

_____

_____

Then, put them in the correct order to find your Magic Message:

_____   _____   _____

_____   _____   _____

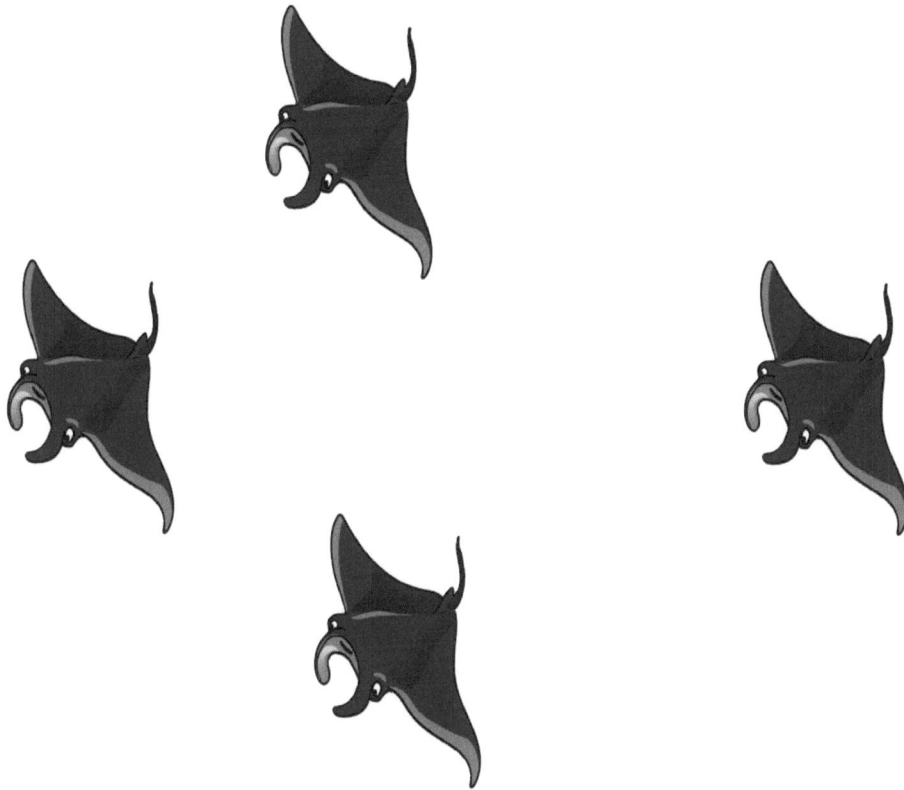

Bonus items to find! Can you find these animals from pages 8-9?

Horse-eye Jack

Scissortail Sargeant

Highhat

Smooth Trunkfish

Squirrelfish

Honeycomb Cowfish

Glasseye Snapper

Kingfish

Redlip Blenny

Foureye Butterflyfish

Queen Triggerfish

Grey Triggerfish

Scrawled filefish

Coney

Creole Wrasse

Trumpetfish

Orange-spotted Filefish

Bar jack

Nassau Grouper

Barred Hamlet Fish

Hogfish

Rock Beauty

Lionfish

Bermuda Chub

Spotted Scorpionfish

Palometa

Clown Fish

Great Barracuda

Can you find these animals from pages 10-11?

Dolphin

Puffer fish

Blue Whale

Humpback Whale

Sheepshead fish

Tiger Shark

Bull Shark

Great White Shark

Hammerhead Shark

Whale Shark

Sawnose Shark

Mola Fish

Oarfish

Krill (tiny shrimp)

Blue Marlin

Japanese Giant Spider Crab

Orca Whale

Dogfish

Can you find these animals from pages 12-13?

Longhorn Cowfish

Flying Fish

Great White Shark

Loggerhead Sea Turtle

Green Sea Turtle

Leatherback Sea Turtle

Red-footed Booby

Wilson's Storm Petrel

Red-billed Tropic Bird

Campbell black-browed mollymawk

Octopus

Brown Skua bird

Blue Petrel

Slender-billed Prion

Bulwers Petrel

Can you find these animals from pages 14-15?

Grouper

Tuna

Dragonfish

Hatchetfish

Frilled Shark

Cuttlefish

Pelican Eel (aka Gulper Eel)

Goblin Shark (aka Goblin Fish)

Manta Ray

Vampire Squid

Giant Squid

Blobfish

Anglerfish

Can you find these animals from pages 20-21?

Beluga Whale

Bowhead Whale

Greenland Cod

Greenland Shark

Walrus

Atlantic Cod

King Crab

North Pacific Giant Octopus

Two-horn Sculpin

Arctic Flounder

Sea Lion

Pacific Herring

Porpoise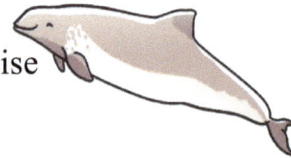

Puffin

Snow Seal

What else is in the Ocean?

The animals, fish, reptiles, mollusks and plants found on these pages are a tiny part of life in the oceans!

Can you think of other living things found in them? Write them below:

Bonus Feature:

Many classic novels feature ships or boats in the oceans. They include "The Silent World" by Jacques Cousteau; "Voyage of the Beagle" by Charles Darwin; "Moby Dick" by Herman Melville; and "20,000 Leagues Under the Sea" by Jules Verne. These sea-faring vessels, plus three more, are found in this book; can you find and name all seven of them, and name the novels (and authors) in which they are featured?

Boat	Page	Novel	Author
1.			
2.			
3.			
4.			
5.			
6.			
7.			

How can you help keep the oceans clean?

People sometimes don't know or don't care about how important oceans are. They throw plastics and trash into them, and then the oceans become polluted.

What are some ways you can keep our beautiful, vital oceans clean and healthy for every living thing that calls the ocean their home (and for the rest of us, too)?

A) Wherever you are, recycle every single thing you can, like soda cans, glass bottles, juice boxes, metal cans…even milk jugs and orange juice cartons and yogurt cups can be recyclable.

B) If you can't recycle it, throw all trash away in a trash can.

C) When you're away from home, and you can't recycle your things and you can't find a trash can, pack up everything you have and take it with you to recycle or put in a trash can later. "Pack it in, pack it out", no matter how tiny it is, like cigarette butts, empty sunscreen bottles, napkins, broken toys, etc. Leave nothing behind.

D) All of the above.

E) None of the above.

If you answered "D", you are correct!

Facts about the Oceans

- Water covers 75% of planet Earth. This water is divided up into 5 major oceans, but they all are connected to each other. From biggest to smallest, the oceans are the Pacific, the Atlantic, the Indian, the Southern, and the Arctic.

- The Pacific Ocean covers almost a third of the Earth's surface. Also, it has more than 450 volcanoes surrounding it; they are called the "Ring of Fire."

- The Atlantic Ocean divides North America and South America from Europe and Africa.

- The Indian Ocean is the warmest of all oceans.

- The Southern Ocean is sometimes called the Antarctic Ocean and surrounds Antarctica. The Arctic Ocean covers the North Pole and usually has lots of ice in it.

- The biggest fish in the world is the Whale Shark; they can be nearly as long as a school bus! Like the Blue Whale, they are filter feeders: they fill their mouths with water, then push it back out of their mouths, and the fringe-like material that rims their mouth, called the baleen, strains the plankton and small fish out; they stay in the Whale Shark's mouth and become their food.

- The Great White Shark is the largest predatory fish in the world. They can be 15 feet long or more, and they eat seals, sea lions, and smaller toothed whales.

- Beaches can be made of sand, pebbles, rocks, cobblestones, or even shells. Sometimes they're really soft to walk on; other times they can hurt your feet! They can be many different colors, too; around the Pacific Ocean, near volcanos, beaches are covered with black sand.

Facts about the Oceans

- The heart of a blue whale weighs about 400 pounds.

- According to the Guinness Book of World Records, the tallest sandcastle ever made was constructed in Connecticut, USA, in May 2011. It was 11.53 m (37 ft 10 in) tall.

- The deepest place on Earth is the Mariana's Trench in the Pacific Ocean; it's nearly seven miles from the ocean's surface down to the bottom! In March 2012, James Cameron (Best Director Oscar for "Titanic") reached the bottom of the trench in a specially designed submersible vehicle he helped create. When he hit bottom, he told his support team that the area looked very lunar, or moon-like. It took him 1 ½ hours to get back to the surface.

- Some words we use today were created from work or play in the oceans. SONAR stands for Sound Navigation and Ranging. SCUBA stands for Self-Contained Underwater Breathing Apparatus.

- Phytoplankton are little microscopic organisms that float at the ocean surface and, through photosynthesis, create almost half of the world's oxygen.

- Horseshoe crabs have lived on Earth for 450 million years. Jellyfish have been around even longer, for almost 500 million years!

- The Box Jellyfish, which lives in waters around Asia and Australia, is considered the most poisonous animal in the world.

- One of the most famous and worst ocean-based disasters in history was the sinking in the North Atlantic Ocean of the "unsinkable" RMS Titanic in April 1912. Hitting an iceberg on her maiden voyage from England to New York City, the ship took on water, cracked in two, and sank in just over 2 ½ hours; more than 1500 people lost their lives.

What's the Difference?

1. How are seals different from sea lions? How do walruses compare to seals and sea lions?

2. How are porpoises different from dolphins?

3. How are whales different from sharks?

Everyone has a story to tell!

Which beaches have you visited?

Which ocean was at each of the beaches you visited?

What was the ocean like at each one? Was it cold or warm? Was the water blue, or grey, or green?

What animals did you see?

What plants did you see?

What reptiles or mollusks did you see?

Was the beach free of trash?

Would you go back to that beach? Why or why not?

What's the Difference? Answers:

1. Seal lions, seals and walruses all have fins for feet. Sea lions have large flippers; seals have small flippers. Sea lions are brown; seals can be several different colors. Sea lions bark loudly, "walk" on land using their flippers, and have visible ear flaps; seals are quieter, wriggle on their bellies on land, and (usually) lack visible ear flaps (only fur seals have ear flaps). Walruses, both male and female, have tusks, and are bigger than most seals and sea lions.

2. Dolphins have long "beaks", or noses, that protrude from their body, while porpoises' noses are more part of their overall body structure. Dolphins have sleek, elongated bodies, while porpoises' are more roundish and portly. A dolphin's dorsal fin (the fin on its back) is curved backwards, towards its tail, while a porpoise's dorsal fin is more triangular and upright.

3. Sharks are fish while whales are mammals (people are mammals, too). A shark's skeleton is made of "cartilage"—the bendable material in a human's ears and nose —while a whale's skeleton is made of bone. Sharks have gills on the sides of their bodies to get oxygen from water, while whales breathe in air through a "blowhole"- an opening in the top of their heads. Sharks are cold-blooded and stay warm through the water temperatures in which they swim, while whales are warm-blooded; they can control their internal temperature.

ABOUT THE AUTHOR

After an education and career in geographic science, KAREN FULKERSON is pursuing a dream she has harbored for 15 years: developing books for all to enjoy, but particularly designed with reluctant readers in mind. Why? She wants to help these students increase proficiency in, and enthusiasm for, reading. This ambition is a direct result of raising a son who didn't enjoy reading in elementary school.

"Oceans!" is Karen's first entry in the Kayful Books non-fiction activity-based book series, and her second professional writing endeavor. Residing with her husband in Virginia, Karen loves travelling (bucket list: visit all 61 U.S. National Parks), adopting rescue pets (currently has four kitties), drinking a good margarita, collecting seashells, and attending every Def Leppard concert she can.

Karen can be reached at: kayfulbooks@gmail.com, www.facebook.com/kayfulbooks, www.instagram.com/kayfulbooks.

ABOUT THE ILLUSTRATOR

GUS MORAIS is a professional illustrator residing in his home town of Sao Paulo, Brazil. Born in 1983, Gus earned his degree in Advertising from the University of Sao Paulo, Brazil's most prestigious educational institution. He has been working as a visual artist since 2008, publishing artworks for advertising agencies, book publishers and newspapers across Brazil, Europe and the United States. One of his most recent illustrations, featured on the front page of The Washington Post's Christmas 2017 Style section, earned the 2017 Award of Excellence from the Society for News Design's 39th annual "Best of News Design™ Creative Competition. Now the father of a young son, he is thrilled to jump into the world of children's literature!

Gus can be reached at gusilustra@gmail.com, www.facebook.com/gustavo.morais.52687, www.instagram.com/gus_morais/.

www.ingramcontent.com/pod-product-compliance
Lightning Source LLC
Chambersburg PA
CBHW060834270326

41933CB00002B/85